# Software Development: A Case Study

# Executive Summary

## Introduction

Salzburg Software Applications is a start-up end-to-end mobile application developing company located in Salzburg, Austria.

## Purpose

The purpose of this business plan is to offer guidance for the development of a Mobile App development company that will sell applications specific for the Apple iPhone, iPad, and iPod Touch and Android based Smartphones and Tables. This business plan will also showcase the expected financials and operations over the next five years.

## Mission

We bring a personal and effective approach to every project we work on which allow us to innovate in a way that others cannot. And frankly, we don't settle for anything less than excellence in every project.

## Vision

We believe in the simple not the complex. We believe in deep collaboration with our customers and bring a personal and effective approach to every project.

## Opportunity

There is a growing market for smartphone applications that can be sold through Apple App Stores as well as custom-made applications for individual clients. As the usage of smartphones increases, there is a corresponding increase in the demand for new, engaging applications that can serve entertainment and informational purposes. Salzburg Software Applications (SSA) plans to use this growing opportunity to generate revenues by developing smartphone applications for the market.

The growth of the market in the US can provide some indications of the potential for growth in other regions of the world. In 2009, the revenues from mobile applications reached almost $3 billion. It was estimated that the market for mobile applications will increase up to $14 billion in 2014. Mobile application developers will likely have a share of $10 billion out of these revenues.

The regions offering the greatest potential are Africa, Asia and Eastern Europe. Between 2005 and 2010, these markets experienced immense growth. The market for mobile phones during this period grew by 278% in Africa, 218% in Asia and 119% in Eastern Europe. In 2009, 2.6 million applications were downloaded in Asia, which was the largest volume in the world. Being in close proximity to the Eastern Europe market, SSA is well-poised to take advantage of this lucrative opportunity.

Clients are now seeking a complete service package instead of a one-off transaction with the application developer. Hence, there is an opportunity for end-to-end development service where the clients can be guaranteed of the regular maintenance and updating of their applications through dedicated App stores. Our company will offer a complete solution to the app development needs of our clients, right from the background analysis and research to development and after sales support. This includes the stages of prototyping, design, development, testing, app submission, supervision and updates.

The use of smartphones and tablets is increasing rapidly; hence, the opportunity for growth in the smartphone application development market is significant. Recently, there has been a growth in the diversity in the use of smartphone apps, such as in professional fields. Professionals in medicine, tourism, and management are regularly using smartphone apps to meet professional goals.

In line with the growing demand, a number of platforms have emerged through which SSA can sell its products to clients and prospective customers. Among these, Apple and Google offer the most popular platforms that SSA can use. Their high level of popularity makes them a promising marketing and sales channel for SSA.

Since SSA will be based in Salzburg, it is important to note that it will be the only company in the neighboring area to provide a complete end-to-end application development package. SSA will therefore have the first-mover advantage in this region. It is expected that clients will prefer SSA's complete service package over the fragmented services offered by competitors.

Because the Salzburg region is a smaller regional market, SSA will make use of the opportunity to develop applications through third parties. By acting as the app development outsourcing partner for third parties, we will gain valuable experience of diverse customer needs and market trends.

There is an opportunity to enter the German market through outsourcing. Through outsourcing, SSA will target a diverse range of customers in different sectors of the market. We will develop apps that can be used in the fields of financial services, healthcare, retail, media, telecom, and education. Because of this growing demand, clients are coming to expect high levels of customer service, innovation, trust and speed of development that a new firm such as SSA is more capable of providing.

Businesses in diverse industries are realizing the potential of smartphone apps to expand their business. Apps enable businesses to reach out to their clients on their smartphones by providing them useful information as well as opportunities for entertainment. New services can also be developed for clients specifically through customized apps. The apps will be developed for clients in enterprise, financial services, consumer retail, and media sectors as these would enable the clients to offer regular information updates, status reports and transaction management services to their customers. Customers' high needs to organize their information and manage daily activities have made smartphone apps an indispensable tool for ordinary consumers. Apps are being used to regulate indoor heating systems, pay bills, learn new languages and play games while travelling on the bus.

Customers are coming to expect to receive a personalized service that meets their unique needs. SSA would possess the required expertise and attitude towards customer service to offer the required balance of personalized service and efficiency.

Mobile apps are currently being developed along the lines of three popular models. These are known as the premium model, the freemium model and the ad networks model. Under the premium model, the client has to pay a download fee to get the application. A number of firms are using this as the simplest model to generate revenues through direct sales of their applications to the customer. At the same time, this is an expensive model as the cost barriers are high. Only 14 percent of the total app downloads from the Apple app store are based on the premium model (Xyologic, Aug 2012).

The freemium model overcomes some of the challenges of the premium model in that the customer gets to download the app for free. However, this is a simple barebones version of the app and does not offer a lot of functionality. However, the app does offer content for purchase within the app so that the customer may upgrade to a version with greater functionality and features. The upgraded version comes at a cost that goes to the app developer. This is a more popular model than the premium model.

Advertising has made inroads into the app development market. The ad networks model allows the customer to download the app and all its features for free. The software developer earns revenue when the customer clicks on an advertisement displayed on the app screen. The pay-per-click model means that profit margins are relatively lower compared to the premium and freemium models. At the same time, the software developer can select advertising partners and charge different rates for displaying the ads in prominent places on the app. In this way, the potential for earning greater revenues is increased.

Another growth opportunity for app developing companies lies in developing content in regional languages. Particularly in developing countries that are experiencing a growth in the technology usage but where proficiency levels in English remain lower than in developed countries, there is a growing demand for apps offering content in regional languages (Deloitte, 2013).

Developing apps has become a common activity among university students and app enthusiasts. However, clients are recognizing the value that a professional app development company with high standards of performance can bring to the table. These factors present a highly favorable environment for SSA to enter the app development sector.

## Solution and Business Model

Salzburg Software Applications (SSA) will maintain its competitive edge over its rivals while pursuing the attractive growth opportunities offered by the market. On the strength of its technical competence and effective marketing, SSA will cater successfully to the needs of the market and expand into new territories.
SSA will focus its strengths on the development of applications for smartphones and mobile phones. The solutions devised by the company will serve entertainment needs as well as important business functions for the clients and users. The apps developed by the company will be compatible with the iOS and Android platforms, which are the most common platforms used in smartphone technology. The iOS applications will work on devices such as iPads and iPods, while the Android compatible apps will run on smartphones and tablets.
While the primary emphasis will remain on developing apps for the end consumer, SSA will also offer app development services to third party clients. These activities will supplement the revenue base of SSA and enhance its financial strength.

The business model of SSA will thus be built upon a two-pronged approach where the company will develop proprietary apps under the SSA brand while offering outsourcing services to third party clients at the same time.
In pursuing its business objectives, SSA will offer end-to-end app development services to clients. The entire process covering the stages of requirement analysis, background research, prototyping,

design, development, testing, app submission, app supervision, support and updates will be performed by the trained and competent employees of SSA. This will give us greater control over the entire process. In addition, the customer will be facilitated to procure all the development services through a single point of contact with SSA. The business model will further enable SSA to provide its services to clients in a range of industries and sectors, including but not limited to financial service providers such as banks, retail organizations, media services providers, and healthcare providers. SSA will develop apps with the functionality to add value to the business functions of our clients, especially those functions that affect the quality of service experienced by their customers.

Once the customer has been brought on board, SSA will receive a set of requirements from the client and will initiate the reiterative process of designing and developing the app. The client will be engaged at every stage of the process and his feedback on the performance of the test versions will be incorporated in subsequent versions until the final version is approved. The inclusive approach of the SSA team and the commitment of the employees to make the client feel valued will enhance the effectiveness of the final product. Each project at SSA will be treated as a unique activity that offers enriched experiences to users as well as the employees working on the project. The timelines and resources will be determined for each project independently. It is likely that some projects may take four weeks to complete while others may take up to six months. Hence, it is difficult to prescribe a specific period for each project to be completed.

Once approved, each project will be assigned to a team consisting of at least two members. One of these will be a designer and another will be a developer. However, depending on the size of the project, the developer may take over the responsibilities of the designer too and manage the project on his own.

The methods used to develop the apps will incorporate the use of Scrum and Agile software development programs. These are the leading programs for developing software and SSA will obtain the software and develop the employees' competencies in these software. An iterative and incremental approach is used in developing each project. This approach allows changes and corrections to be made on an incremental basis. The feedback from clients can be incorporated before significant costs have been incurred in project development. It helps to maintain flexibility while working towards the project goals.

Each project will also be charged to a project manager who will supervise the development and flow of the project. The project manager will allocate resources to the project and resolve any complaints or challenges during project execution. At times, an appropriate member from the project team may be appointed as the project manager. Depending on the situation, the customer may also delegate an individual to act as the project supervisor. The project manager will also perform the quality assurance function for the project. He or she will see to it that the project is executed according to the requirements specification and the client's feedback. Some organizations often have the CEO performing the role of the project manager. The project manager will also undertake scenario-testing to assess various project risks and develop contingency plans for mitigating these risks.

## Industry Key Success Factors

The application development industry is dynamic and growing at an accelerating rate. The key factors for success in the industry stem from the pressures of constant innovation, functionality and economic profit. Some of the dominant success factors for the industry are discussed below:

Reduced Ambiguity: The mobile app development industry places pressure on the developer firms to incorporate greater certainty into their project plans. It is not uncommon for different stages of the project to be performed by different members of the team working at different locations. Therefore, it is important to have an unambiguous set of explicit requirements so that members do not have to make any assumptions. The client's requirements and project parameters should be defined in clear and explicit terms.

Greater Stability: For a mobile app development project to be successful, the company should incorporate greater stability into the project design and management. Again, in situations where the project is being executed by disparate teams, stability reduces the need for frequent communication and redesign. When such redesign or change in the specification of requirements occurs, it becomes necessary to ensure that the changes are communicated to all the members working on the project. These costs can however be avoided if the project specifications are determined after careful analysis and are not changed unnecessarily.

Platform compatibility: As the number of smartphone users increases across the world, software developers and app developers are scrambling to produce software that can work on multiple platforms. At the same time, smartphone manufacturers are encouraging new platforms to be developed so that they can lock in their customers and prevent them from switching over to rivals. Hence, selecting which platform the application is to be compatible with is a crucial decision for the app developer. It is important to exploit the growing market potential by developing apps that are accessible to maximum numbers of users and can be run on several different platforms.

Customer Service: Customer service is crucial to survival in the mobile app development industry. At times, clients do not have a clear picture of what they want. At times, they do not come in with a specific budget in mind, which makes things difficult for the developer. High levels of customer service can ensure that clients are engaged in such a way that they develop a realistic set of expectations and requirements. Customer service is also important during the development stage as it helps to keep the client informed and involved in the development phase. Finally, after sales customer service is essential to stimulate sales and obtain feedback.

Dependencies: Dependencies play an important role in the success of mobile app development projects. Dependencies may arise during the same project and between different projects being executed by the same company. Resources may have to be shared by the different projects and employees. Critical path method and other project management tools should be employed to manage dependencies and allocate resources efficiently. The critical path method can also help the project manager to manage temporal dependencies in the project. Coordination: Effective and smooth coordination among the team members is essential for project success. Especially with teams where the members are spread over geographical distances, coordination is essential to avoid bottlenecks and pileups. The team members need to share information regularly with one another and with the project manager. At the same time, they require information about updates and changes in specifications without any loss of time. Hence, the project success for mobile application developers depends on the flow of information and communication systems developed by the company.

Vertical Integration: For success in the mobile app development industry, the companies need to be vertically integrated as far as possible. Particularly for companies located in the developed markets, vertical integration is important as it can help to reduce costs. Companies that are not vertically integrated face challenges from rivals who outsource the development function to low labour cost countries. Effective vertical integration can enable the firm to perform most of the functions in-house and offer better quality through greater control over the development process.

Technology: Latest technology and devices are essential for success in the mobile app industry. Innovation, productivity and performance depend to a great extent on the tools and technology that are used to develop products. Project management software such as Basecamp and others are also being used to provide greater control over the project execution. Equipment such as laptops and desktop computers are essential for executing the project and developing designs. Application development and design tools are also required as they determine the quality of the product.

Workforce: Competent and motivated employees are the backbone of the mobile app developer firm. Each team member needs to be equipped with industry standard skills and high levels of motivation. The firm needs to invest in their training and education. At the same time, it is important to ensure that labour turnover is kept to a minimum.

## Company Overview

Salzburg Software Applications (SSA) was founded in 2013 in the town of Salzburg, Austria be Cornel MICU. The company is staffed by an in-house team consisting of project planners, project managers, app developers, designers and testers. The company develops mobile apps for clients in different industries and markets. SSA aims to become the leading innovative developer of mobile apps in the industry. The company has been incorporated and registered as a limited liability company in 2013. The company has been granted a license to operate its business in Austria. The legal name of the company is Cornel MICU BSc who is the founder and owner of the company. The company headquarters are located at Baslestrabe 10/3, 5020, Salzburg, Austria.

The company will serve clients within its established markets. These markets cover the territories of Austria and neighboring Germany. The location of the business is partially advantageous because it is located close to the German market which is a strategic advantage for the company. However, there are some disadvantages of locating the company in Salzburg. The cost of living is high which will ultimately affect the cost of production and remuneration of employees. Secondly, most of the local businesses are related to the tourism sector, which offers limited potential for the mobile app developer. Finally, the town does not have a large number of trained and skilled app developers, which means that the employees will have to be relocated to Salzburg, adding more to the costs of human resource. The company offers services to enterprise clients as well as end consumers. The enterprise clients will be served in Salzburg and in Bayern area of South Germany. End consumers will be served internationally through App stores across the world. Currently, the mobile apps developed by SSA are compatible with the Android software used in Apple smart devices. However, the company is planning to develop apps that are also compatible with the Windows platform.

## Marketing Strategy

SSA will operate under a carefully developed marketing plan that will enable it to raise awareness about the company's services among the target customers. The primary customers of the company are the businesses and companies who are looking towards making information available to their customers over mobile platforms. SSA will market its services to companies who want to incorporate mobile applications as a means of increasing their sales. The marketing plans will initially be implemented in Austria as the immediate focus will be on Austrian companies. In later stages, the company will expand its marketing activities into Germany and the surrounding markets.

SSA will develop informative marketing content that highlights the customer needs our products can satisfy. On the basis of this information, our prospective clients in our target markets will contact us. The following marketing strategies will be employed to reach out to the customers:

Word of Mouth: SSA is a small organization; hence, there are insufficient resources to engage in above the line advertising and marketing strategies. Moreover, SSA is catering to the business buyer, which means that there is a greater need for personalized communication rather than mass media advertising. SSA will market its services through positive word of mouth generated by current customers. Word of mouth marketing will have greater credibility and will leverage the strength of existing business relationships among our prospective clients.

Social Network Marketing: SSA will use social networking websites to market its services to its target customers. Many companies are developing business profiles on social networking sites such as Facebook, Twitter and LinkedIn. This helps them to maintain regular profile throughout the year and also allows them to engage directly with their customers. The strategy will enable the company to use a variety of social channels and media to promote their services and applications to customers.

Merchandise: SSA will use promotional merchandise as part of its marketing strategy. The promotional merchandise will consist of items that can be distributed as gifts among prospective clients and will include key chains, stationery, mugs, and so on. The merchandise will be branded with the SSA logo. Where possible, a brief message explaining the profile and services of the company will be provided along with the website address of the company. The merchandise will be distributed during sales visits, trade fairs and other promotional events. These methods will offer greater exposure to the company and inform our clients of our services.

Website: Most of the marketing function will be performed through the official website www.salzburg-software.com. The website will be developed in line with the current trends in search engine optimization so that the website appears prominently in search engine listings. Information will be organized to facilitate the visitor in finding the information that they need. This approach will help the company to gain more exposure and acquire enquiries from first-time clients. SSA will also approach related websites to offer our links to be hosted on a reciprocal basis. This will increase the company's exposure among international clients as well as local clients.

Direct Marketing: In a business-to-business environment, it is important to undertake direct marketing to develop long-term relationships with clients. SSA will also pursue direct marketing to inform clients about its services and professional strengths. SSA leaders and managers will network with other professionals in the industry, collaborate in funding university research along with other companies, and interact directly with satisfied customers to learn about their experiences. The company managers will also write informative articles for trade publications such as magazines like c't and heside.de to build a positive and dynamic profile in the industry.

Promotional videos: SSA will develop a promotional video detailing the activities and services performed by the company. This video will be produced and transmitted to existing as well as prospective clients. The video will also be uploaded to the company website to be accessed by the general public. The purpose of this video will be to generate curiosity and engagement with customers by providing information in an interesting format. The managers and key officials of the company will explain the various functions and highlight the core strengths of the company. Undoubtedly, the message delivered by the top leadership will have a greater impact on the target audience.

Face-to-Face Sales: Personal visits and cold calling will be an important aspect of the company's marketing strategy. The importance of personal face-to-face interaction in business relationships is undisputed. SSA representatives will visit prospective clients and explain how the company can develop high quality solutions that meet their business needs. Prospective clients will first be identified and then an appropriate marketing plan will be developed for each client accordingly keeping in mind their clientele, markets, products, services and technological resources. Regular follow up visits will also be conducted to offer maintenance and after-sales support.

Email marketing: This will be part of the online marketing strategy that will also include website marketing described earlier. SSA will develop an emailing list of key organizations in the various sectors we will target. Promotional email messages will be sent to these prospective clients informing them about the company and its services. These emails will have to be sent frequently because of the vast number of emails received by prospective clients every day. However, care will be taken to avoid flooding inboxes with unwanted email messages that could create a negative perception about the company.

## Industry and Market

The mobile app industry is developing at an accelerating pace around the world. It is a global industry with operating centers spread across continents. It is also a technology driven and technology enabled industry, which helps it to maintain flexibility in a global and dynamic environment.

The competitive landscape is highlighted by both small as well as large developers. This indicates that financial resources are not a significant barrier to entry of new firms. However, technical knowledge and expertise is, which is why only firms with competent employees and resources can enter the industry and sustain their position. Established brands that may enter the industry include Apple and App store, Nokia and Google's app store. Access to resources and funding is relatively easy which explains a large number of new entrants each year.

This poses some challenges as well as opportunities for new firms like SSA. Since SSA will focus on developing mobile apps for vendors such as Apple and others, it is crucial for the company to diversify its clientele to avoid the threat of its customers becoming its competitors. To achieve this end, small mobile app developing companies are exploring relationships with independent clients and companies by developing bespoke solutions for their needs. This strategy will help the companies to increase the switching costs for customers and strengthen their position in the competitive environment. In addition, the firms are also expanding into other service areas such as web solutions and multiple platforms for their clients.

The industry is highly competitive because of the relatively low barriers to entry and high threat of substitutes. These competitive pressures have motivated several companies to compete on a cost basis by offering their services at the lowest possible rates. To achieve this, operational centers have been established in countries with low operating costs such as India and Malaysia. In response to this strategy, smaller and more flexible companies are focusing on customer relationship management as a strategy to overcome their cost disadvantage with innovation, flexibility and responsiveness to the client. Companies are now focusing on their ability to be adaptable and flexible. In doing so, they are dedicating resources towards developing customer relationship management competencies in addition to technical competence.

Despite the intensifying rivalry, the mobile app industry continues to grow and the customer base also continues to increase. With the widespread proliferation of smartphones and other mobile computing devices, the potential for growth in the industry continues. Although more challenging, firms continue to maintain high levels of profitability because of the low operating costs and large number of customers. It should also be noted that the industry is still at a nascent stage. As the industry develops and new technologies are brought to the market, there is potential for further diversification and introduction of new services. Customer needs may enhance and they may demand newer forms of entertainment and information. Therefore, it may be said that the potential for growth in the industry is significant for all players.

The performance of firms in the mobile app industry is not affected by suppliers to a great extent. There is generally a low bargaining power of suppliers in the industry. Apart from the technical equipment there are few other essential supplies that companies require to set up their business. Consequently, there are a number of suppliers, both local as well as global, who offer the same or similar equipment at attractive rates. Hence there is little room for suppliers to collude or fix prices among themselves.

There are more than ten mobile platforms including the popular Android and Google platform that app developers can choose from; although this is largely determined by the client or customer. The development of online sales channels has further made it more convenient for app developers to procure resources and equipment at competitive rates. There is a tendency for suppliers to lock in customers by offering warranties and service agreements. These arrangements can restrict the flexibility and independence of app developers to some extent, but it also offers greater certainty and assurance of continued service.

The app development industry is relatively new and has not yet matured fully. Therefore, as the industry develops, there is an increased likelihood of consolidation and greater coordination among the suppliers. Moreover, the online environment is likely to eliminate cost differences among various suppliers, making it more likely for them to focus on service quality and specialization in certain niche segments. Overall, the suppliers do not pose significant threats at present.

The strongest factor affecting the success of firms in the app development industry is the increasing power of buyers or customers. The buyer wields unprecedented power because he or she has the power to directly download the app to their smartphone. In addition, buyers are often influenced by word of mouth promotion. Therefore, the marketing efforts of a mobile app developing company may be ineffective if the existing customers are not satisfied with the product. Despite this risk, the growing numbers of buyers attracts more firms to enter the industry and claim their share of the increasing pie. More than 10.5 billion downloads take place every year, which averages to about 4 app downloads per smartphone customer. There is also immense pressure on app developers to innovate consistently and keep a tab on changing customer needs and trends among users. The industry trends show that users have less loyalty towards specific apps or app developer companies. Hence, a successful app is no longer a guarantee of the success of the next app by the same company.

In addition to word of mouth promotion, app users are also influenced by the websites of app stores. Thus, it is necessary for app developers to develop some kind of communication channel with the users so that they can be informed and persuaded about the attractiveness of certain apps. By sharing information with users and helping them make informed purchase decisions, app developer companies can effectively manage the high bargaining power of buyers in the industry.

App developers are highly susceptible to substitutes taking over their market share. Given that the average life of an app is not very long until better apps are developed, the consequences of losing out market share to substitutes can be crucial. A large number of mobile app developers have proliferated the market by developing apps for various platforms. These apps can be developed at low cost and made available to the users instantly. Hence, the firms have to be on their toes at all times to respond to the growing threat of substitutes in the industry. The best way of responding to these threats is by using innovation and creativity to develop new apps for the market. Constant scanning of the market and competitors is vital for survival and growth of any firm in the industry.

Because of the low costs of development and the flexibility afforded by the Internet and other technology, the prices offered by substitutes are similar to the original product, which again limits the scope for competitiveness available to individual players. In addition to price, the substitutes are also similar in terms of user-friendliness, convenience and security. Many of the apps are developed for the same platforms. As a result, the apps offer more or less similar functionality and user experience. It is suggested that importing an app from one platform to another requires only 45% incremental effort, which also makes it easier for apps developed for one platform to pose competitive threat to the apps developed for different platforms.

The mobile app industry is characterized by constant change. Since the emergence of the iPhone in 2007, the appetite for creative smartphone apps has skyrocketed. Consequently, a large number of mobile app developing companies have entered the industry and are vying for a share of the app user's pocket. Apps ranging from games to financial management tools are being churned out by developers every day. Businesses are finding that offering apps to their consumers allows them to provide more value-added services and increase their customer base. The launch of the App Store in 2008 provided a convenient channel to app developers for delivering their product to the consumers. Since then, the market and the technology have developed rapidly, making it a challenge for those in the industry to determine the direction in which the industry is heading.

As the market matures and a clutter of apps fills up the market space, there is going to be an increased demand for creative and relevant apps. The smartphone is fast becoming a necessity rather than a luxury. This change has occurred as a result of the greater applications of smartphones in daily life. As the future becomes more mobile, companies will be forced to offer greater functionality and useful features with their apps. Customers are likely to pay premium value for apps that help them with important tasks such as data management, using appliances and making transactions. Firms investing in such ideas are more likely to ride the wave in the coming years.

A number of environmental factors also affect the mobile app industry. In the legal environment, there are issues relating to user data privacy and confidentiality. Therefore, app developers have to be careful when they require users to share personal data through the app with other users. The data should be secure when used through the app. Economic factors are less important because most apps are well within the reach of the ordinary consumer. Smartphone technology is also becoming more affordable as rates go down and cheaper versions of smartphones become available in developing markets.

Another challenge for the industry is the limited scope for selling apps through multiple channels. At present, the Apple App Store is the largest channel available to app developers to sell their products to consumers. The entire ecosystem operates as a closed eco-system in the hands of the private sector. This makes penetration into the ecosystem difficult, except through the authorized gatekeeper of the proprietary network. Another similar channel that is not as large but certainly growing rapidly is the Google Play Store. In order to break into this market, it is necessary for the apps to conform to the specifications and criteria of the Apple and Google stores. This again imposes a constraint on the creative freedom of the app developing company. Every app is reviewed for compliance and is approved only if it conforms to the requirements of the store owner. These barriers are likely to persist over the immediate term as there does not seem to be a likelihood of alternative channels emerging.

Competition is a major challenge in the mobile app industry. Because of low barriers to entry and lucrative profits to be made, there is a large number of competing firms in the industry. It appears that a mobile app can be developed anywhere from a dormitory room to an Internet agency. A dedicated mobile app developer company like SSA has to deal with these competitive pressures from several directions. The most appropriate response to these competitive challenges is to strengthen the workforce by recruiting highly skilled and motivated developers and designers. Experienced project managers also play an important role in the success of the mobile app firm.

In addition to competitive threats and the power of buyers, the industry is also characterized by increasing opportunities for collaboration between mobile app developers and marketing organizations. Mobile app developers generally lack the resources to engage in their own marketing while large clients like Apple and Google are not likely to market the suppliers in their promotional campaigns. Hence, individual marketing companies can play a vital role in the success of mobile app firms. In addition to marketing the products of the firm in the market, these marketing partnerships can also be helpful in securing business for the firm. Thus, it may be seen that mobile app developing firms collaborate with marketing companies to get new clients and orders. These measures enable struggling firms to secure business and establish themselves in the competitive and uncertain industry.

The smartphone is the foundation of the mobile app industry. As the smartphone becomes more accessible, it is highly probable that the demand for mobile apps will increase, thus increasing the market for new firms. The greatest growth is likely to be experienced in Eastern Europe, Asia and Africa as developed markets face saturation and stagnant demand. Firms that have close access to and understanding of user trends in these markets are more likely to experience success in these markets. Furthermore, technological developments such as the introduction of 3G technology in developing countries and 4G technology in developed countries create greater possibilities for development and innovation in the industry. Service standards are likely to be enhanced as a result of which companies that are well-resourced in competent and technically sound developers will be more successful than others.

The growth certainly lies in developing markets where a growing middle class with western sensibilities aspires to adopt western consumption habits. As the markets of China and India open up to the mobile app industry, there is going to be greater demand for apps in the regional languages. This will require recruitment of employees well-versed in the local language and culture of these markets. While this will promise more opportunities for growth it will also pose challenges in human resource management and market research. Firms may find that they have to develop their cross-cultural sensitivity to reap the benefits of a rapidly globalizing industry.

## Key Members of the Company/Management

Cornel Micu is the founder and chief director of Salzburg Software Applications. He possesses the technical competence and business acumen to develop SSA into a leading mobile app developer in the region. He possess a bachelors degree in engineering from the Salzburg University of Applied Sciences. He was worked as a mainframe software developer in Raiffeisenbank where he performed diverse tasks to develop banking software for the organization. He has also previously launched a startup organization with a partner by the name of Location Aware Automation. It used the GPS of the smartphone to automatically regulate home heating systems. He is fluent in both German and English and has strong leadership and motivating skills.

Ioana Micu is one of the co-founders of SSA. She completed her bachelors in hospitality and tourism management from University College Birmingham in 2012. Ioana is responsible for the marketing and sales functions. At the moment, she is holding a number of positions at SSA including Marketing and Sales Director and Assistant Operational Manager. She is fluent in the use of office software and hotel management software such as Fosse, Marsha and Opera. She can speak Romanian, English and Spanish. She possesses strong customer management skills and cross-cultural sensitivity.

Damaris Walter is the chief operating officer of SSA. She possesses relevant qualifications and experience to make her the ideal person to look after operational aspects of the company. She possesses strong technical knowledge and leadership skills to maintain a productive and satisfied workforce.

PWT Neudorfl acts as the chief financial officer and accounting consultant for the company while Dr Sluka Hammerer is the legal consultant.

## Competition

There are no significant competitors operating in Austria; however, the mobile app industry is a global industry and competition can emerge from any part of the world. Some of the leading mobile app developers in the world are located in the US and UK. The firms that can directly compete with SSA are those that operate on a flexible operating model such as SSA.

Mubaloo is one of the leading mobile app developer companies in the UK. The company was established in 2009 and comprises its own team of planners, managers, developers and designers. All the operations are carried out in-house which gives greater control to the management. The company has developed more than 160 mobile apps for clients in a number of different sectors ranging from financial services to healthcare and telecom. Mubaloo provides end-to-end service delivery and develops apps that are compatible with Android, Windows and HTML5 systems.

Fueled is a New York based mobile app developer that offers customized mobile app services to diverse clients. The company also has offices in Chicago and London which enables it to cater to the needs of clients in these markets. The revenues of the firm have amounted to $250,000 and the company has developed several successful applications in the past few years. The company caters to established corporate clients as well as startups. Fueled specializes in developing customized solutions for each customer. In addition to app development services, Fueled has also moved into the branding and design sphere by offering these services to its clients. Apart from developing mobile apps for iPhones and Android operating systems, the company offers website development services. The company promises increased revenues for its clients in addition to lower bounce rates, increased number of transactions and convenience. The company has won a number of awards for its service delivery and high standards of performance.

Y Media Labs is a media app developer based in San Francisco, USA. This company also offers a complete suite of mobile app design services. Y Media Labs is led by Ashish Toshniwal who is the CEO of the company. The company also specializes in other areas of mobile services including mobile strategy and mobile application design. Y Media Labs develops applications for clients in different industries and helps them offer greater functionality to their clients on different platforms. Y Media Labs develops apps that are compatible with iPhone and iPad technology in addition to the Android operating system. Some of the apps developed by the company include children's educational apps, word puzzle games, photography apps, and credit management apps. Some of the notable clients of this company include ebay, the BBC, PayPal and Bank of America. Financial information of the company was not available on the website to make an assessment of its financial strength.

Sourcebits is another San Francisco based company that offers mobile app development services to large as well as small clients. The company has been operating since 2006 and enjoys the financial support of venture capital firms. Some of the notable clients of the company include Coca Cola, Hershey's and P&G. The company has operating offices in North America, Europe and India which allows it to serve clients in the major growth regions of the world. The company is also able to maintain round the clock communication with its clients as a result of its presence in three continents. The company has been rated favorably by Lead411 and other industry experts. Since its inception in 2006, the company has developed more than 500 apps and web solutions for its clients. More than 20 apps developed by Sourcebits have made it to the top ten ratings across app stores.

Dev Experts Team is a mobile app development company based in Germany. It is a much smaller company compared with other competitors discussed here and is closest to SSA in terms of scope and market. The company develops mobile apps for educational purposes, websites and other web-based systems. The products developed by the company are compatible with iPhone and Android technology. Around seven team members make up the company which helps it to maintain flexibility. Like SSA, Dev Experts also provides end-to-end solutions while keeping the client involved at each stage of the development process. The company also guarantees that any bugs discovered in the product will be fixed by the team at no additional costs.

The analysis of the competitors shows that innovation and dependable quality are the most important competitive strengths of successful companies in this industry.

## Competitive Advantage

The competitive advantage for SSA is that it is the only specialized mobile application developer in the Salzburg region. This promises a huge potential for the company to emerge as the leading service provider in the region and extend its influence into more lucrative neighbouring markets. The company abides by a strong set of social values which will ensure that SSA is accepted in the local as well as international community as a committed and responsible organization. SSA will sponsor employees willing to take part in social missions in different parts of the world. The company has already demonstrated its commitment to corporate social responsibility by sponsoring one of its employees on a mission to Africa. SSA has collaborated with World Vision to achieve this aim. The company also sponsors social causes through various sports and community activities.

In addition to the location of the business, SSA will derive competitive strength from the ability of the company to offer end-to-end solutions to customers. Our entire development process is automated which enables us to perform at high levels of efficiency compared to the competition. The highly trained and experienced workforce not only distinguishes SSA from the competition but also ensures that SSA will develop products in close alignment with the needs and expectations of the client. At SSA, we believe that we do not do anything different from the competition, but we do it in a better and more efficient way. This allows us to offer superior quality to our clients while earning attractive profits for the company.

## Conclusion

The main source of funding for SSA will be the owner's equity. The owner will invest from his personal savings into the venture. The funding will be used to finance the office space, employee salaries, and other operating expenses. The funding has already been incurred and the owner plans to finance all investments up to EUR 30,000 from his personal savings. Friends and family members have also pledged their support for the venture.

SSA will use the funding from owner's equity to finance the startup costs and other working capital requirements. In case the investment exceeds EUR 30,000, additional funding will be sought through bank loans. Because SSA has been established as a private limited company, it will not offer shares to the general public. All the profits will be retained in the business and will be sued to finance growth and expansion of the company.

The funding will also be used to maintain adequate levels of cash reserves to meet the operating needs of the business as they arise. In addition, the working capital will be maintained to meet the expenses of maintaining the head office at Salzburg, meet overhead expenses and pay salaries to the employees. As profits are reinvested in the business, the company will be able to undertake stronger marketing, serve a greater number of clients, and acquire the latest technology. The company will also use funds to sponsor the training and education of its employees. This will enhance their competence and efficiency, which will lead to improved quality and more revenues for SSA. The company will also require the employees to sign a bond with the company prior to any training stating that if the employee resigns from the company within a year after the training is complete, he or she will reimburse the company for the amount of the training fees.

The company will pursue an exit strategy if the management decides not to continue the venture any further. The management will liquidate the assets or sell the venture to an investor when the company has acquired a significant valuation. To attain a high valuation, it will be necessary for the firm to earn consistently high profits in the initial period. The company could be acquired by a large mobile app developing company looking to invest in the Eastern European region. Because the market also borders the German market, it is likely that the business will receive a good valuation as long as the operations are profitable and the company has an attractive client profile.

The owner will seek a productive and mutually beneficial relationship with all lenders and investors. The fact that the owner has invested personal equity in the business would be a positive sign of his personal commitment to the venture and his objective of seeing through the business to success.